Inside Eye™

BIG BUILDINGS
OF THE
ANCIENT WORLD

BOOK HOUSE
a SALARIYA imprint

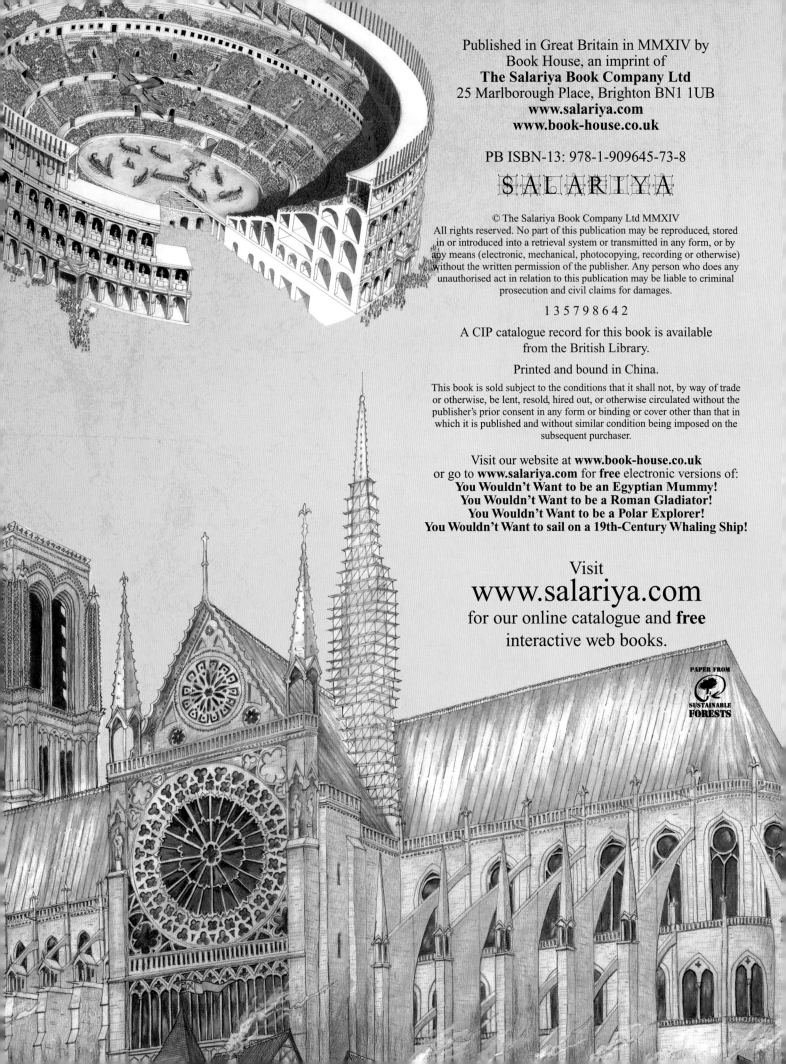

Published in Great Britain in MMXIV by
Book House, an imprint of
The Salariya Book Company Ltd
25 Marlborough Place, Brighton BN1 1UB
www.salariya.com
www.book-house.co.uk

PB ISBN-13: 978-1-909645-73-8

SALARIYA

1 3 5 7 9 8 6 4 2

A CIP catalogue record for this book is available
from the British Library.

Printed and bound in China.

Visit our website at **www.book-house.co.uk**
or go to **www.salariya.com** for **free** electronic versions of:
You Wouldn't Want to be an Egyptian Mummy!
You Wouldn't Want to be a Roman Gladiator!
You Wouldn't Want to be a Polar Explorer!
You Wouldn't Want to sail on a 19th-Century Whaling Ship!

Visit
www.salariya.com
for our online catalogue and **free**
interactive web books.

PAPER FROM
SUSTAINABLE
FORESTS

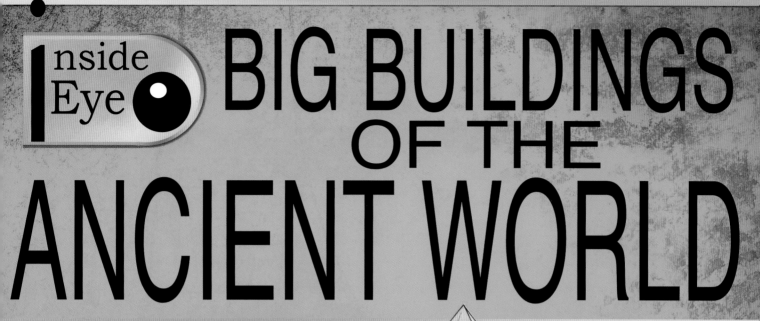

BIG BUILDINGS OF THE ANCIENT WORLD

Written by Dan Scott

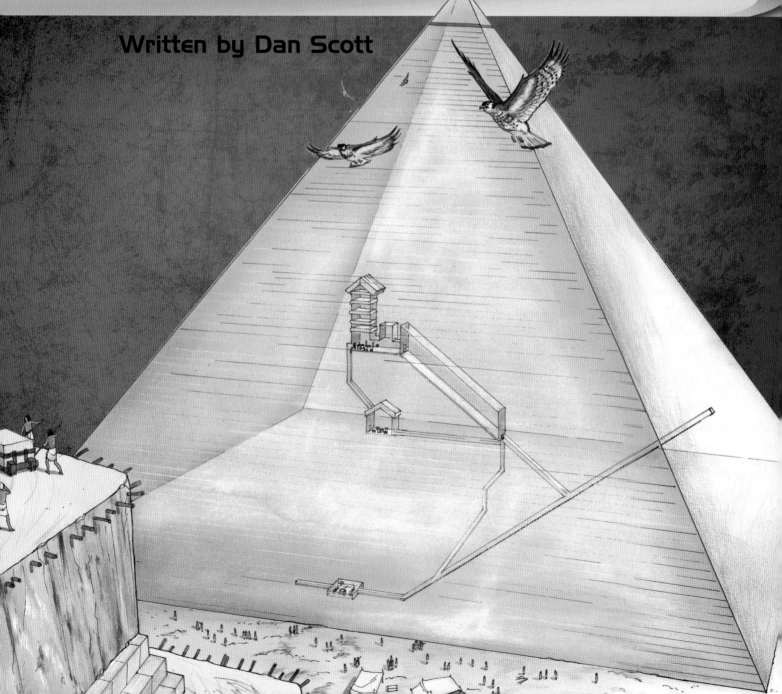

CONTENTS

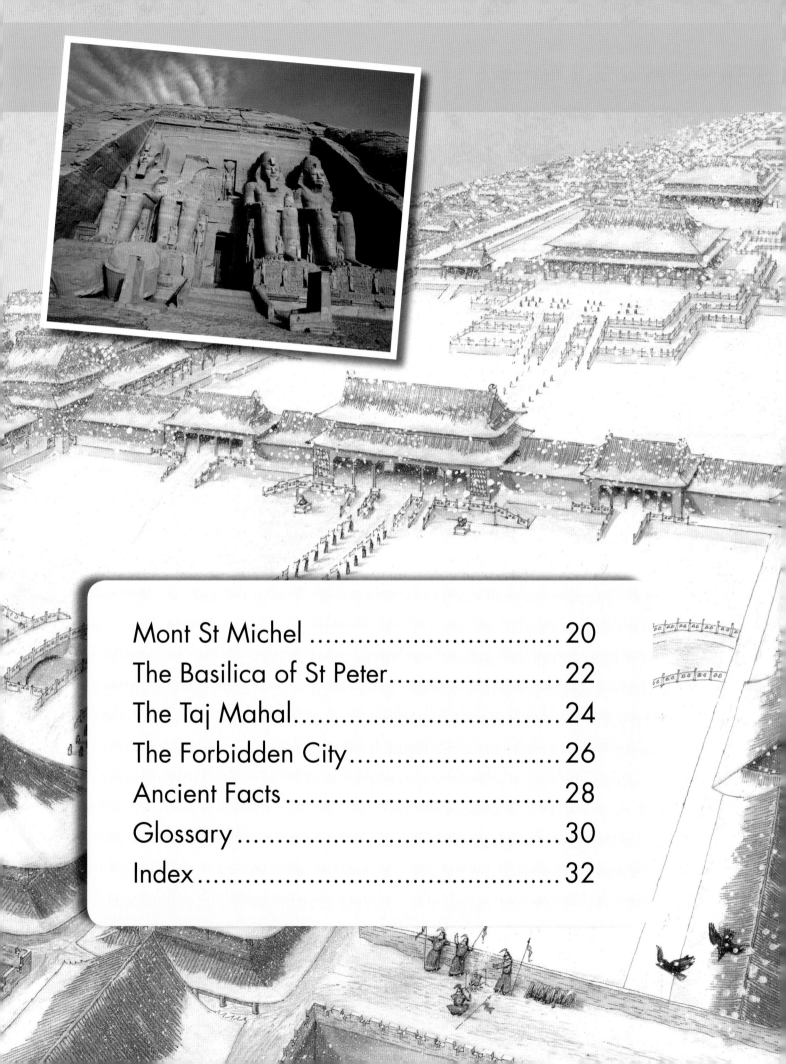

Great Buildings

The world is full of buildings, where we live, go to school, shop and do many other things. Some buildings are different. They stand out because they are so big and so beautiful. They might be palaces, churches, castles or even gigantic tombs. Many of these amazing buildings were created in ancient times – long before cranes, diggers or any other mechanical tools existed.

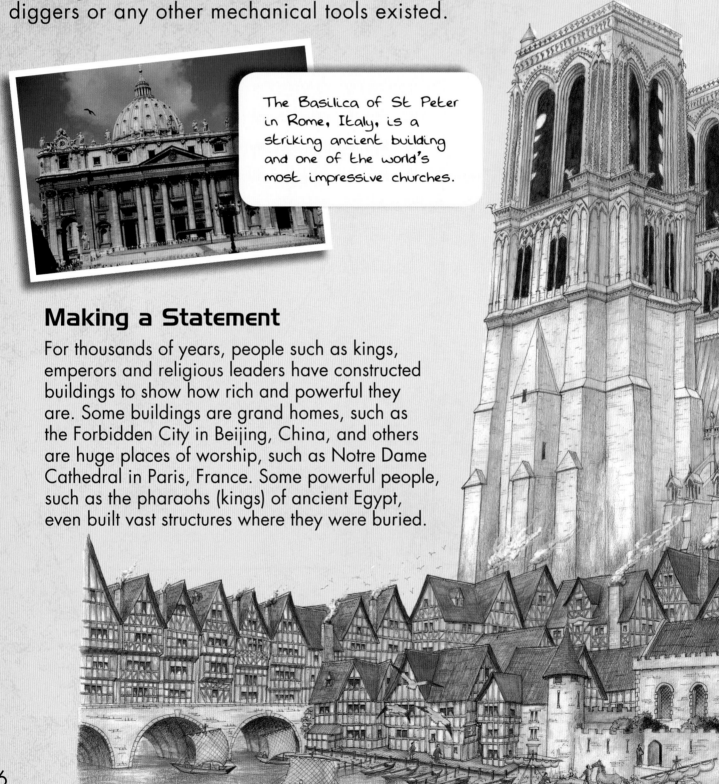

The Basilica of St Peter in Rome, Italy, is a striking ancient building and one of the world's most impressive churches.

Making a Statement

For thousands of years, people such as kings, emperors and religious leaders have constructed buildings to show how rich and powerful they are. Some buildings are grand homes, such as the Forbidden City in Beijing, China, and others are huge places of worship, such as Notre Dame Cathedral in Paris, France. Some powerful people, such as the pharaohs (kings) of ancient Egypt, even built vast structures where they were buried.

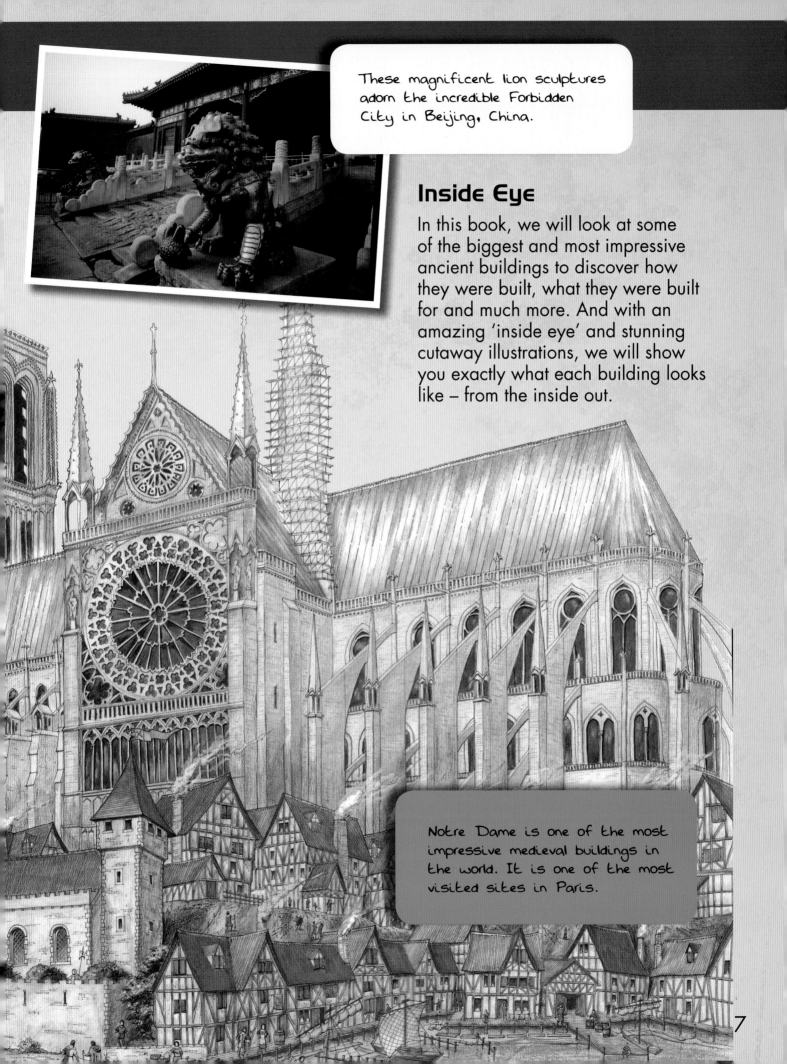

These magnificent lion sculptures adorn the incredible Forbidden City in Beijing, China.

Inside Eye

In this book, we will look at some of the biggest and most impressive ancient buildings to discover how they were built, what they were built for and much more. And with an amazing 'inside eye' and stunning cutaway illustrations, we will show you exactly what each building looks like – from the inside out.

Notre Dame is one of the most impressive medieval buildings in the world. It is one of the most visited sites in Paris.

Notre Dame

Paris in the twelfth century was a busy trade and cultural centre. Its old cathedral church was out of date and too small for a population of nearly 100,000. A new bishop, Maurice de Sully, wanted a grander building in the fashionable new Gothic style. So, in 1163, the old cathedral of Paris was demolished to make room for one of the first and most beautiful of the Gothic cathedrals – Notre Dame.

Arch

Notre Dame took 100 years to build. The two towers, completed in 1250, are 68 m high. Their square tops and lack of spires were unusual for a medieval cathedral.

Centre of Attention

Notre Dame was a vital part of town life. It was one of the few public buildings in medieval Paris, so people went there every day to worship, to look at the cathedral's beautiful carvings and stained-glass windows, and even to shop and trade.

Creepy Creatures

High up on Notre Dame are hundreds of grotesque stone-carved creatures called gargoyles. They are, in fact, waterspouts, used to drain water from the gutters.

Gothic Style

A Gothic church had pointed arches and ribbed vaulting, like a rib cage of arches that supports the roof. The outward thrust of the roof vaulting is transferred to flying buttresses, a series of freestanding stone pillars connected to the building by arched structures. The Gothic style created incredibly strong but beautiful buildings.

Spire

South rose window

Flying buttress

The Gothic building system allowed architects to build higher, thinner walls, which created space for large stained-glass windows.

The cathedral window designers made use of natural light to enhance the colours of the magnificent stained-glass windows. The warm tones of the southern sun complement the red glass that dominates the south rose window, built in 1260.

The Great Pyramid

About 5,000 years ago, the ancient Egyptians developed the art of building with cut stone. The first pyramid was built around 2700 BC as the burial place for the pharaoh Zoser, and many more pyramids followed over the next 1,000 years. The largest pyramid, built for the pharaoh Cheops around 2560 BC, is the Great Pyramid at Giza, near modern Cairo. It is still the largest stone building in the world.

Back-breaking Work

A workforce of about 4,000 men built the Great Pyramid. It took 20 years to complete, using 2,500,000 stone blocks, with an average weight of 3 tonnes. This amazing feat of engineering was achieved using only ropes, levers, wedges and a few stone and copper hand tools.

The Egyptians had no way of lifting the huge stones, so they dragged them up earthen ramps built in tiers along the sides of the pyramid.

The Great Pyramid covers an area of about 5 hectares and was originally just over 147 m high. Four of Europe's largest churches could sit within the area it occupies.

Into the Next Life

A pyramid was a tomb for a pharaoh. His mummified body was placed in a burial chamber, hidden deep inside the pyramid, alongside all the things he would need in the afterlife, such as food, clothes, weapons, furniture and jewellery.

Pharoah's burial chamber

Passageway

The pyramid shape represented the rays of the sun falling on the Earth. After death, the pharaoh was believed to climb heavenwards on the sun's rays.

Dressed for Death

When a pharaoh died, his body was mummified. The internal organs were removed and stored in jars, and the body was left in natron (a type of salt) for 40 days, to dry out. It was then bound tightly in resin-soaked linen and put in a coffin.

Abu Simbel

In 1250 BC, when the Great Pyramid at Giza had already stood for more than 1,000 years, pharaoh Ramesses II ordered a magnificent temple to be built at Abu Simbel, in southern Egypt. The temple was to commemorate the thirtieth year of his reign. It was carved into sandstone cliffs above the banks of the River Nile. Four giant figures of Ramesses, each more than 20 m high, guarded the entrance.

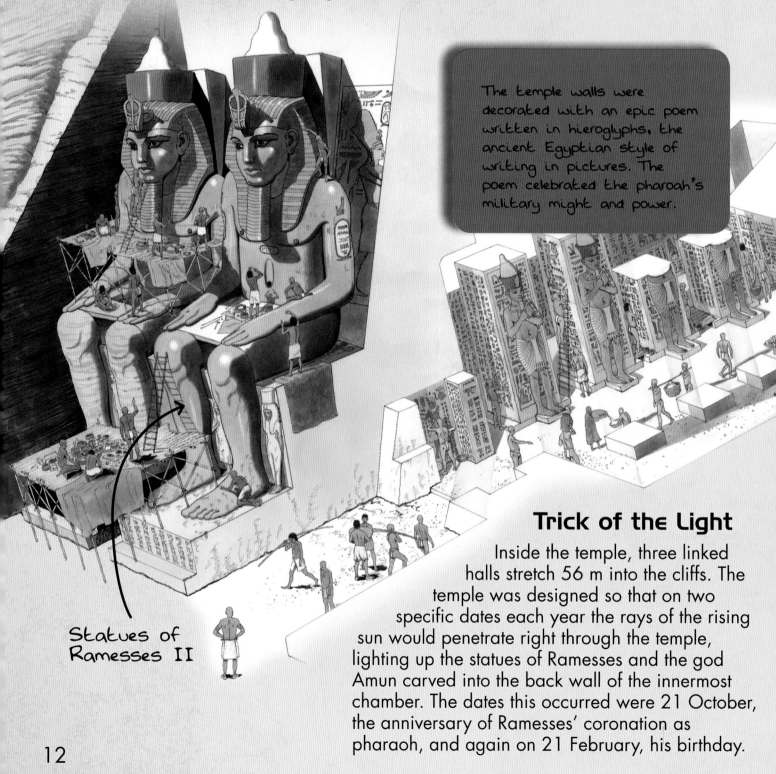

The temple walls were decorated with an epic poem written in hieroglyphs, the ancient Egyptian style of writing in pictures. The poem celebrated the pharoah's military might and power.

Statues of Ramesses II

Trick of the Light

Inside the temple, three linked halls stretch 56 m into the cliffs. The temple was designed so that on two specific dates each year the rays of the rising sun would penetrate right through the temple, lighting up the statues of Ramesses and the god Amun carved into the back wall of the innermost chamber. The dates this occurred were 21 October, the anniversary of Ramesses' coronation as pharaoh, and again on 21 February, his birthday.

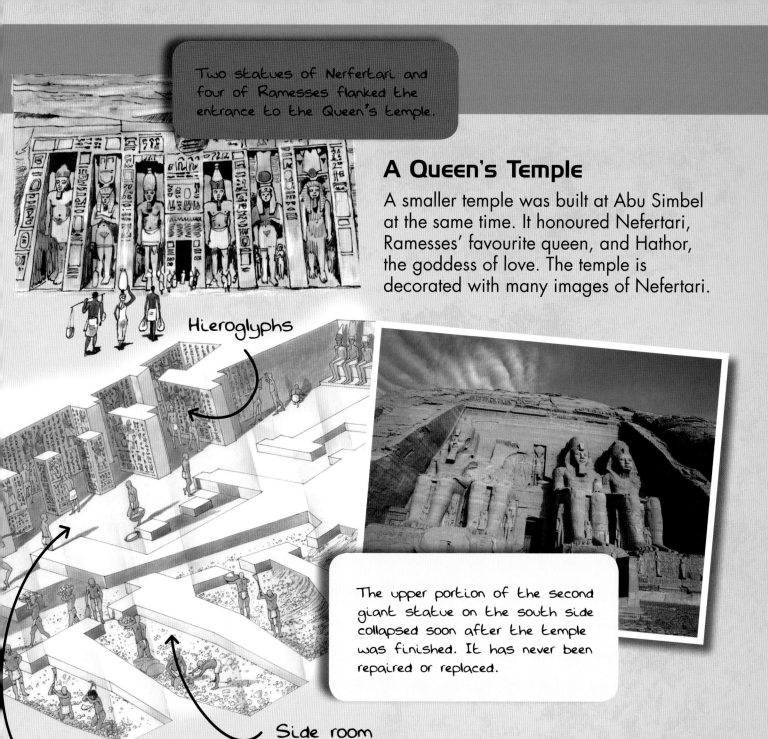

Two statues of Nerfertari and four of Ramesses flanked the entrance to the Queen's temple.

A Queen's Temple

A smaller temple was built at Abu Simbel at the same time. It honoured Nefertari, Ramesses' favourite queen, and Hathor, the goddess of love. The temple is decorated with many images of Nefertari.

Hieroglyphs

The upper portion of the second giant statue on the south side collapsed soon after the temple was finished. It has never been repaired or replaced.

Side room

Cutaway showing the temple interior

Water Works

Boats sailed up the Nile bringing men and equipment to start work on the royal temple. Everything had to be transported by water to this isolated place on the edge of civilisation.

The Parthenon

In 480 BC, Persian forces invaded the Greek city of Athens and destroyed the sacred temples of the Acropolis, or 'high city'. When the Persians were finally defeated in 449 BC, Pericles, the leader of Athens, started to rebuild the Acropolis, including the Parthenon – the temple dedicated to the city's patron goddess, Athena Parthenos.

Perfect Harmony

The Parthenon was a simple structure – a series of vertical pillars, called columns, and horizontal stones, or lintels, bridging the gaps. The number and position of the columns followed strict rules that applied to all Greek temples. In the Parthenon, however, these rules were further refined to create an amazing sense of balance and harmony.

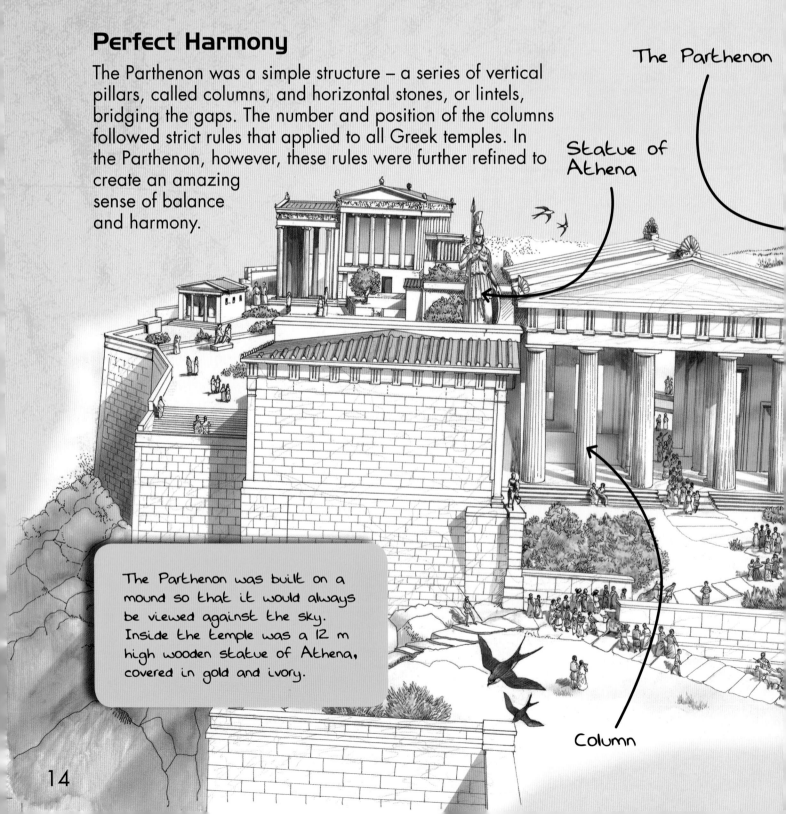

The Parthenon

Statue of Athena

Column

The Parthenon was built on a mound so that it would always be viewed against the sky. Inside the temple was a 12 m high wooden statue of Athena, covered in gold and ivory.

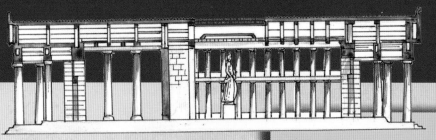

Temple Plan

Columns surrounded the Parthenon. The building within the columns comprised two chambers with a walkway surrounding it. The longer eastern chamber, which housed the statue of Athena, had two rows and two tiers of columns. The western chamber had four tall columns and housed the temple treasures.

The temple had no windows. Some sunlight penetrated through the thin marble tiles that covered the timber roof.

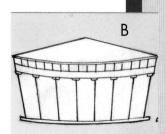

In 1801, the Turks occupied Athens and allowed the British diplomat Lord Elgin to remove large sections of the Parthenon's decorative stonework. They became known as the Elgin Marbles and are now on display in the British Museum in London.

Fooling the Eye

The straight lines of the Parthenon (A) are actually an optical illusion. If everything really were straight, the building would look out of proportion (B). To compensate, the Parthenon was built with sloping corners and tapering columns that lean in slightly (C).

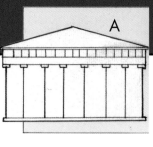

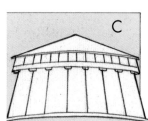

The Colosseum

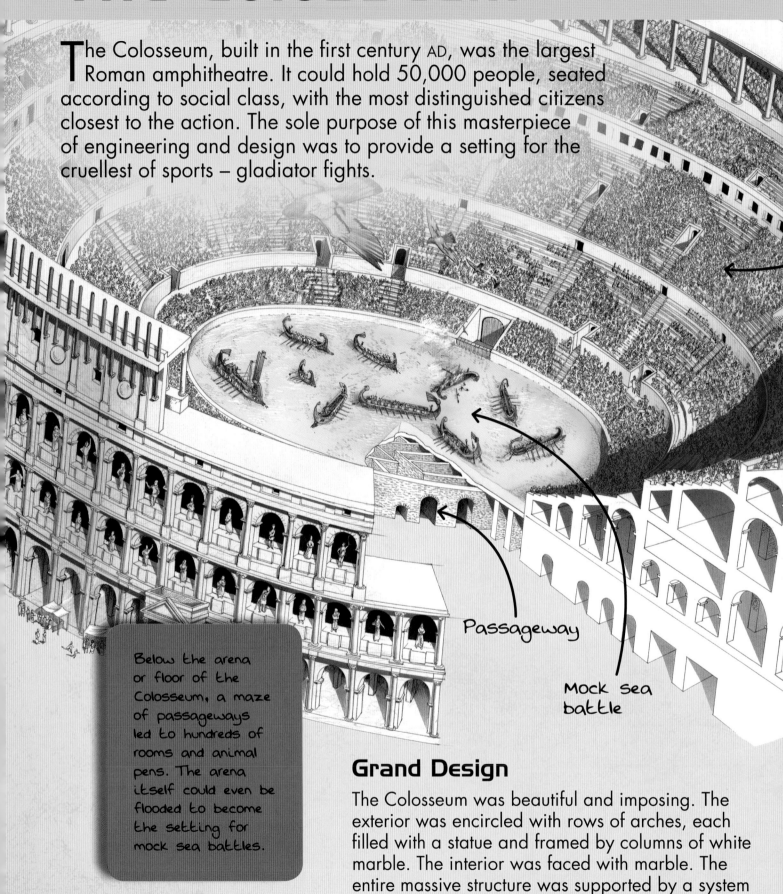

The Colosseum, built in the first century AD, was the largest Roman amphitheatre. It could hold 50,000 people, seated according to social class, with the most distinguished citizens closest to the action. The sole purpose of this masterpiece of engineering and design was to provide a setting for the cruellest of sports – gladiator fights.

Passageway

Mock sea battle

Below the arena or floor of the Colosseum, a maze of passageways led to hundreds of rooms and animal pens. The arena itself could even be flooded to become the setting for mock sea battles.

Grand Design

The Colosseum was beautiful and imposing. The exterior was encircled with rows of arches, each filled with a statue and framed by columns of white marble. The interior was faced with marble. The entire massive structure was supported by a system of arches and arched ceilings, called vaults, which formed the foundations of the seats.

Visor

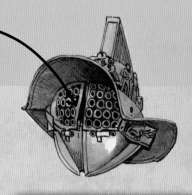

Audience

Fight to the Death

Thousands died in the arena for the entertainment of the Colosseum audiences. Fights between gladiators lasted until one of them was badly wounded. A brave fighter was sometimes spared. However, if the Roman emperor gave the thumbs-down sign, the winning gladiator had to kill his opponent.

A gladiator's helmet had a pierced visor to protect his face, but that made it difficult to see.

The arch was the Romans' greatest building innovation. It was much stronger than the Greek system of columns and lintels and allowed the construction of much bigger buildings.

Emperor Builder

The Roman emperor Vespasian began work on the Colosseum in AD 72, on the site of a lake in the grounds of the palace of his predecessor, Nero. Vespasian died in AD 79, a year before his son, the emperor Titus, opened the Colosseum.

Bodiam Castle

A medieval castle was a fortified stronghold that provided shelter for a lord and his family. Bodiam Castle, in southeast England, was one of the last medieval castles to be built. Completed in 1388 using the latest features of castle design, it was a grand residence as well as a strong fortress. Its living quarters were extremely comfortable by fourteenth century standards.

Castle Life

A small community of about 150 people lived in Bodiam Castle. They included the lord, his family and their personal attendants, knights and soldiers, officials to manage the castle and estate, and workers to maintain the castle. Bodiam had all it needed to survive a siege – a well for water, gardens to supply food, beehives for honey, livestock for meat, and poultry for eggs.

Great hall

Towers were essential for strengthening and defending the 2 m thick castle walls. Round towers were stronger than square towers.

Beehive

Castle gardens

Pretend Castles

By the end of the fourteenth century, the powerful cannons that could demolish thick walls began to make castles obsolete. However, many pretend, or 'bogus', castles appeared in later centuries as splendid residences, such as Schloss Neuschwanstein in Germany, built for King Ludwig of Bavaria in the nineteenth century.

18

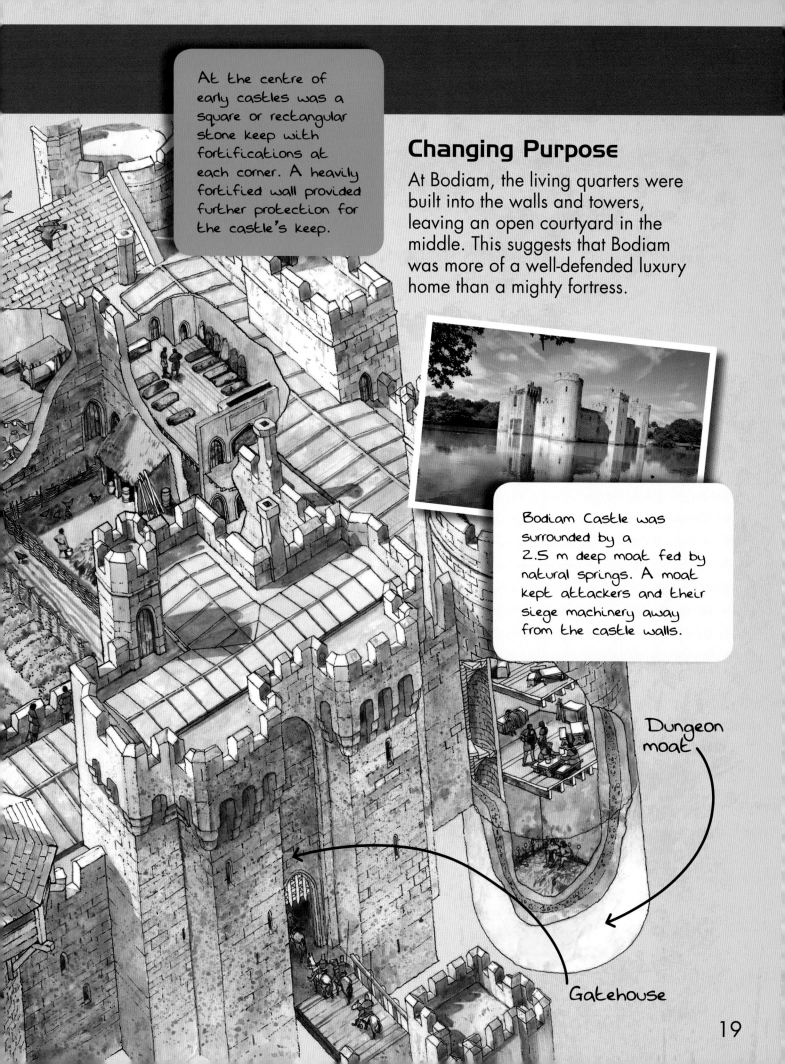

At the centre of early castles was a square or rectangular stone keep with fortifications at each corner. A heavily fortified wall provided further protection for the castle's keep.

Changing Purpose

At Bodiam, the living quarters were built into the walls and towers, leaving an open courtyard in the middle. This suggests that Bodiam was more of a well-defended luxury home than a mighty fortress.

Bodiam Castle was surrounded by a 2.5 m deep moat fed by natural springs. A moat kept attackers and their siege machinery away from the castle walls.

Dungeon moat

Gatehouse

Mont St Michel

Mont St Michel, on the Normandy coast of France, has been a place of pilgrimage since the eighth century. In the eleventh century, Benedictine monks arrived and began to build a church on the summit of the island. The summit is only a quarter of the size of the church, so massive foundations had to be created on all four sides. Two monasteries, built to serve the church, cling to rocky cliffs on the north and west sides.

Monastery Marvel

The walls of the monastery on the north side of Mont St Michel rise 40 m from the island bedrock. The building is such an amazing architectural achievement that it has become known as *la Merveille*, meaning 'the marvel'. The monastery was built in the grand Gothic style, with pointed arches and vaulted ceilings.

The kitchen and storerooms were on the lowest level because all supplies, including water, had to be hauled up from the ocean.

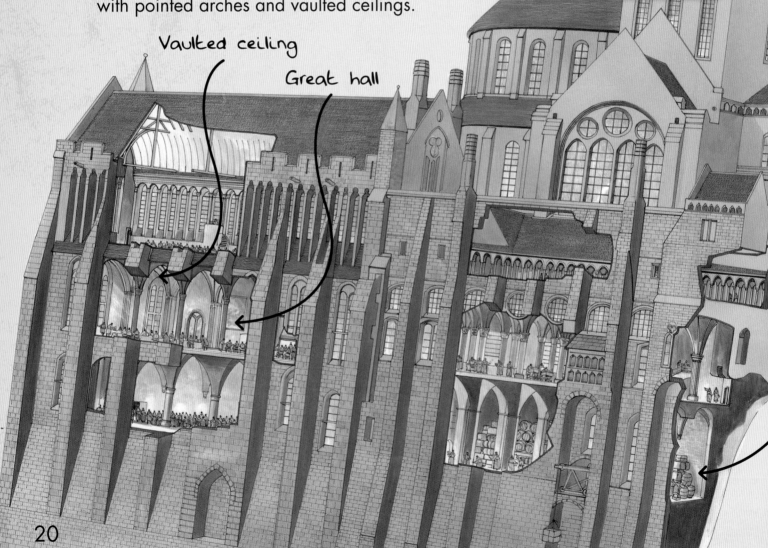

Vaulted ceiling

Great hall

Pilgrim Island

When the tide was high, pilgrims arrived at Mont St Michel by boat. At low tide they crossed a narrow strip of land that connected Mont St Michel to the mainland. Islanders guided the pilgrims across the invisible and dangerous quicksands.

Pilgrims travelled to Mont St Michel to seek the blessing of Michael the Archangel, who, according to legend, ordered a shrine to be built on the site of the island.

A town grew up around the church and monasteries on the island. Over time, other buildings have gradually surrounded most of Mont St Michel.

Storeroom

Patron Saint

Mont St Michel is named after Michael the Archangel, the patron saint of warriors. He is said to have defeated Satan and thrown him out of heaven.

The Basilica of St Peter

The Basilica of St Peter is one of the most magnificent churches ever built and the finest example of Italian Renaissance architecture. Renaissance means 'rebirth' and refers to a return to Greek and Roman forms of art that began in early fifteenth century Italy. The main features of a Renaissance church are a dome and semi-circular Roman arches and vaults.

A Giant Rises

The original St Peter's stood for more than 1,100 years before it was demolished and a new church begun in 1506. St Peter's is largely the work of two Renaissance architects – Donato Bramante and Michelangelo Buonarroti. Bramante died in 1514 before he could carry out his plans. Michelangelo took over in 1546 and designed the dome we see today. The church was finally finished in 1626.

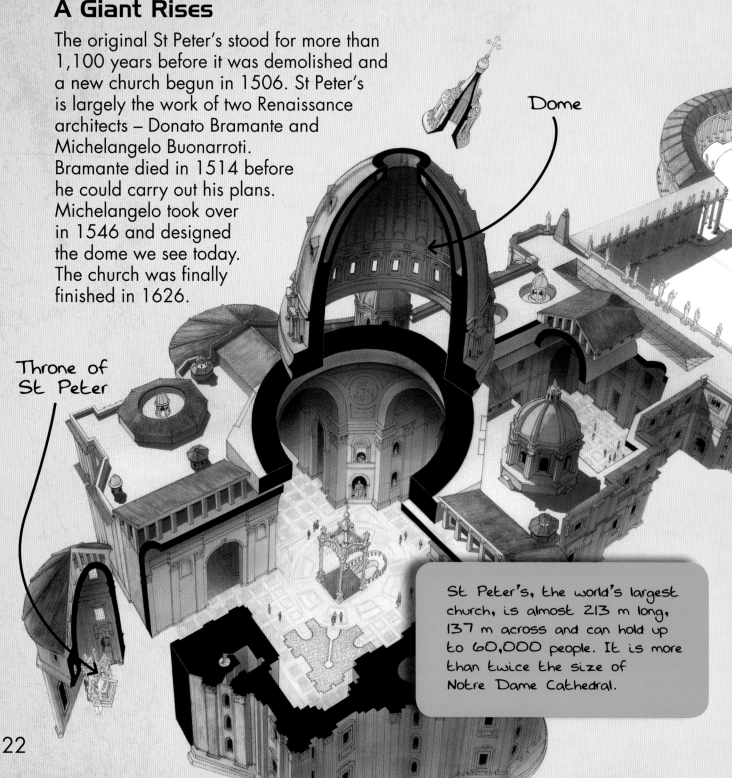

Dome

Throne of St Peter

St Peter's, the world's largest church, is almost 213 m long, 137 m across and can hold up to 60,000 people. It is more than twice the size of Notre Dame Cathedral.

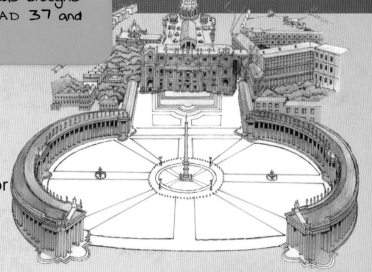

The pink granite obelisk in the centre of the piazza is 25 m high. It was brought to Rome by Emperor Caligula in AD 37 and placed in the piazza in 1586.

Grand Square

Curving around the piazza, or square, in front of St Peter's is a series of regularly spaced columns, called a colonnade. The piazza was designed by the painter, sculptor and architect Giovanni Lorenzo Bernini and was completed in 1667. The statues on top of the colonnade represent 140 saints.

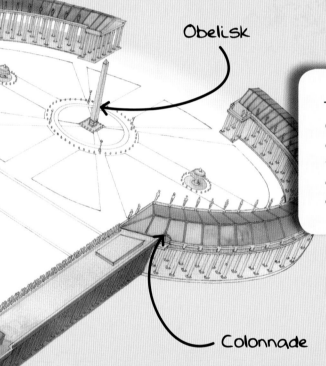

Obelisk

Colonnade

The tip of the cross on top of St Peter's dome is nearly 137 m from the ground. The dome has an inner diameter of 42.5 m.

Cross Paths

The main architects of St Peter's, Bramante and Michelangelo, both wanted the basilica to be built in the shape of a Greek cross, with four arms of equal length. After Michelangelo's death in 1564, however, the main body of the church was lengthened to form a Latin cross.

23

The Taj Mahal

Love and grief inspired the building of the Taj Mahal, close to Agra in India. In 1631, Shah Jahan, an Indian emperor, was heartbroken by the death of his wife, known as Mumtaz Mahal, which means 'Chosen One of the Palace'. He wanted her mausoleum to be more beautiful than anything ever built. The white marble tomb became known by another version of his wife's title – Taj Mahal, 'Crown of the Palace'.

Labour of Love

More than 20,000 people, including workers of precious metals, stone cutters, carvers and inlayers, were employed at the site of the Taj Mahal, which took 22 years to complete. The building incorporated traditional features of Islamic architecture, such as pointed arches and high towers, known as minarets.

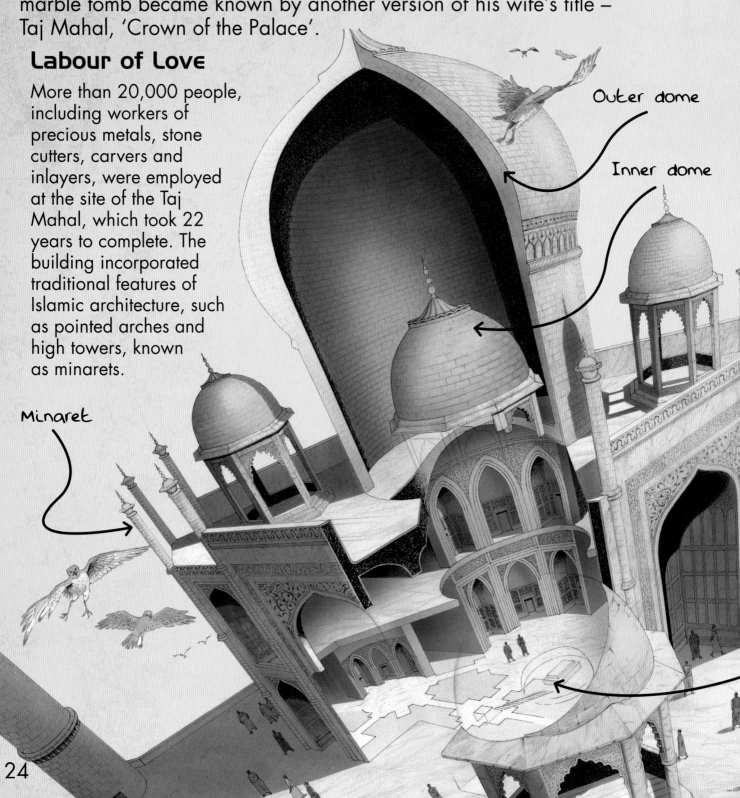

Outer dome

Inner dome

Minaret

The two minarets are used to call the faithful to prayer.

Double Dome

The Taj Mahal is a perfectly proportioned and symmetrical structure built of white marble and decorated with inlaid semi-precious and coloured stones. The huge central dome is actually a double dome. The inner dome is almost 24 m high, surrounded by an outer dome that rises more than 44 m. The double construction meant that the exterior dome could be a great height while the interior ceiling was low enough to be easily seen.

The Taj Mahal is set in a large rectangular walled court, almost 600 m long and 300 m wide.

In the very centre of the Taj Mahal is the cenotaph, or monument, of Mumtaz Mahal, with the cenotaph of Shah Jahan next to it. The real graves are in a crypt underground.

Underground tomb

Beautiful Detail

Both the interior and exterior of the Taj Mahal are decorated with geometrical designs, flowing lines and intertwining flowers and leaves in a style known as arabesque, meaning 'Arab style'.

The Forbidden City

Built between 1406 and 1420, the Forbidden City in Beijing was the imperial palace for generations of Chinese emperors. There, the emperor lived in luxury and seclusion in a city that was forbidden, on pain of death, to most of his subjects. The palace was a complex of audience halls and residences, laid out in a rectangular grid pattern and connected by courtyards.

Everything in Harmony

The Forbidden City was divided into two sections. The outer section contained the administrative buildings. The three main ceremonial halls (the Hall of Supreme Harmony, the Hall of Central Harmony and the Hall of Preservation and Harmony) stood on a three-tiered white marble terrace called the Dragon Pavement. The inner section contained the private apartments of the emperor.

Colour was used to mark the different parts of buildings. Platforms were white, pillars and walls were red, and roof tiles were yellow – the colour reserved for the emperor.

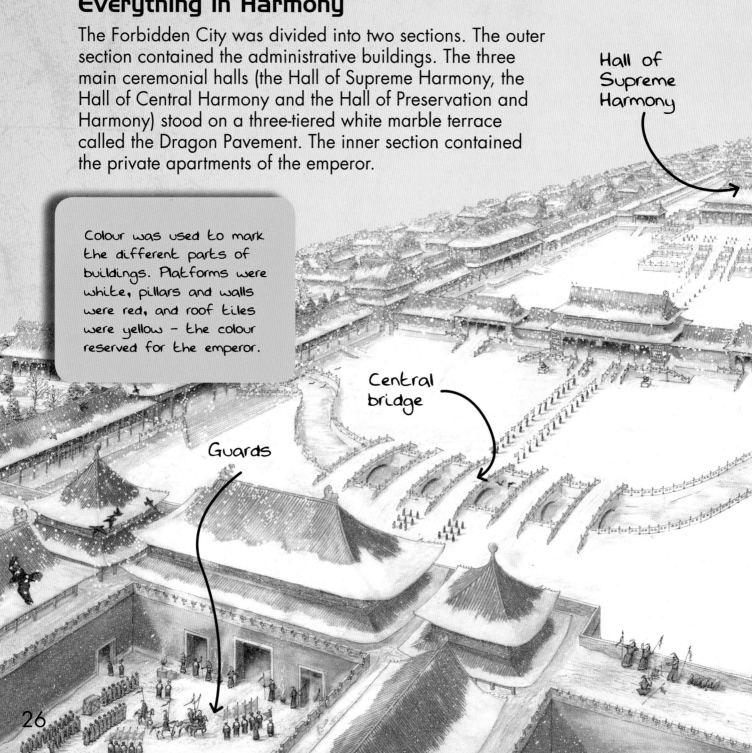

Hall of Supreme Harmony

Central bridge

Guards

The edge of the roof extended outward, well beyond the line of the pillars. The extra weight was carried by an elaborate system of brackets at the end of a column or beam.

Curved Roof

The most striking feature of Chinese buildings was the curved roof. In Europe, roofs had wooden triangular supports that pushed the weight of the roof down through the walls. The Chinese used supporting columns and a series of crossbeams of varying lengths that allowed for shallow curves in the roof. The walls in the Forbidden City were simply screens and not used for support.

Only the emperor could pass through the Meridian Gate, the southern entrance. It was made up of a 60 m long pavilion, flanked by two square pavilions raised on a marble platform, 15 m high.

Guardian Lions

Pairs of bronze lions, one male, one female, kept watch over the gates and the palace buildings. The male's left paw rested on a globe, while a cub sprawled playfully under the female's left paw.

Ancient Facts

Blocked Nose

Before a pharaoh was mummified, the brain was removed through the nose using a special hook.

Higher Ground

In the 1960s, the temples at Abu Simbel were under threat from rising water. Between 1963 and 1968, the temples were cut into 1,050 sections, some weighing more than 30 tonnes. They were then reassembled at a site 60 m higher than the original site.

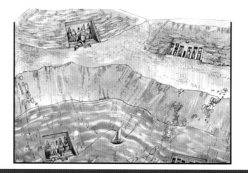

Direct Hit

In 1687, a Venetian army attacking Turkish forces in Athens set off explosives stored in the Parthenon. The explosion destroyed most of the interior walls and killed 300 people.

Tickets, Please!

There were 80 entrances to the Colosseum in Rome. Of these, 76 had numbers that corresponded to numbers stamped on spectators' tickets.

Metal Thieves

The lead spire on Notre Dame Cathedral was melted down to make weapons during the French Revolution at the end of the eighteenth century. The spire was restored in the mid-nineteenth century.

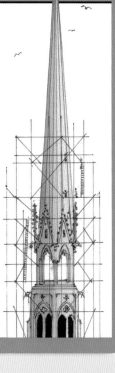

Patient Worker

The sculptor and artist Bernini took nine years, between 1633 and 1642, to create the 29 m tall baldachin, or canopy, over the high altar in the Basilica of St Peter in Rome.

Only Skin Deep

The brilliant white marble of the Taj Mahal is only a veneer. The building was actually made of rubble and faced with marble.

On Your Knees

Court officials reporting to the Chinese emperor at the Forbidden City had to 'kowtow' in submission by touching their head to the floor three times and then lying flat nine times.

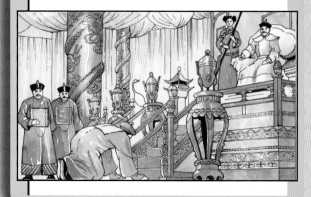

Glossary

Acropolis the upper part of an ancient Greek city where the main temples and monuments were built.

Arabesque a complex design made up of geometric shapes and flowing lines depicting flowers and leaves.

Colonnade a row of columns that support arches.

Crypt a space under a building.

Dome a round roof, placed like an inverted cup over a building.

Flying buttress an arch that starts from a free-standing pier and presses against a wall to take the weight of a vault.

Gargoyle a waterspout carved as a grotesque figure and used to direct rain away from a roof.

Gothic the name given to the style of architecture used throughout western Europe from the thirteenth to the fifteenth centuries. Gothic architecture has pointed arches, vaults and flying buttresses.

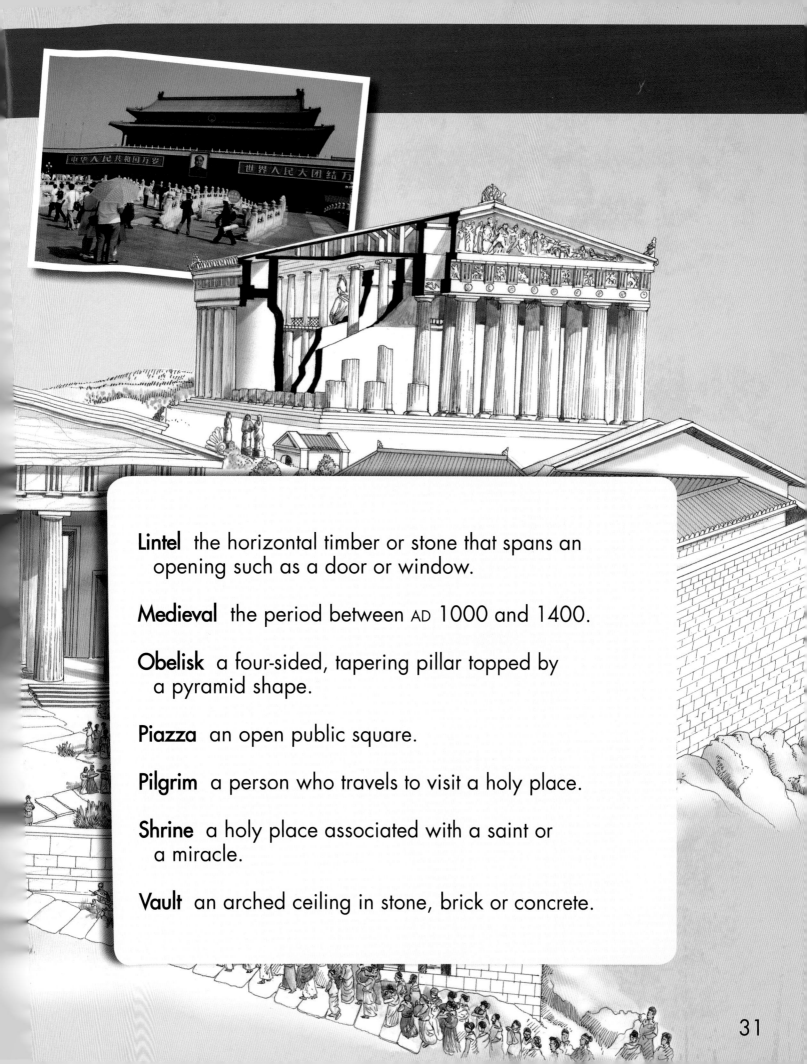

Lintel the horizontal timber or stone that spans an opening such as a door or window.

Medieval the period between AD 1000 and 1400.

Obelisk a four-sided, tapering pillar topped by a pyramid shape.

Piazza an open public square.

Pilgrim a person who travels to visit a holy place.

Shrine a holy place associated with a saint or a miracle.

Vault an arched ceiling in stone, brick or concrete.

Index